A Road to Manhood

By

Stan Howard

A Road to Manhood

Stan Howard

Published by Stan Howard, 2023.

While every precaution has been taken in the preparation of this book, the publisher assumes no responsibility for errors or omissions, or for damages resulting from the use of the information contained herein.

A ROAD TO MANHOOD

First edition. January 13, 2023.

Copyright © 2023 Stan Howard.

ISBN: 979-8227589378

Written by Stan Howard.

Dedicated to River

Dedicated to

River

TABLE OF CONTENTS

INTRODUCTION

Who or what is a man after all? And if I walk a road to manhood will I become a man when I arrive at a supposed destination, say fifty or sixty years of age? A man can be easily defined and becoming a man is more about conquering obstacles in one's path than simply passing mile markers on the road with each passing year. But, it is also about knowing oneself, having the ability to interpret my scars and experiences, offering meaning to my present place of operations as well as direction for yet distant vistas of exploration.

A man is an adult human male. A man is a he just as a woman is a she, each one an image bearer of God in his or her own right, according to the ancient Hebrew Scriptures, differing in sexuality and emotional complexities. God has already placed inside every male all he needs to become a man. I can add nothing to that divine deposit. All I can hope to do in this short pamphlet is "call you up," as a man. It has often been said, "Only a man can call up another man – to hear this call from a woman sounds like nagging in the ears of a male."

Men bear a relationship with their Creator, spouse if married, their children and fellow men and women. As important as work might be, being a man is less about what he does and more about who he is and how he behaves in relationship with others, ruling his own spirit, keeping his emotions under control where needed. An ancient writer offers this wisdom: He who is slow to anger is better than the mighty, and he who rules his spirit, than he who captures a city. [Proverbs 16:32] This proposition speaks to the priority of one's character in relationships over personal achievements. Character and my availability to loved ones and neighbors are more important contributions to community than what I accomplish; this even applies I think in war; for example trust among comrades is more important than medals of valor. This is not to diminish a man's skill set or ability to conquer and arrange his environment; however, if a man's work is not held in balance with relational involvement, especially with his own family, it will destroy any meaningful legacy, leaving but a stone monument or plaque on the wall, attesting to his passage – a phantom that was here – the man I never knew.

Finally, there are two special burdens placed upon men nearly as a birth-right. One of them is positive and the other is negative. One stems from the glory bestowed upon man by his Creator and the other rises from beneath the soles of our feet, urging us to sit down. Men move within a polarity throughout life, positive and negative fields of force which create a basis for our struggles, effecting our dreams and hopes for the future. We can describe this as our participation in the struggle between good and evil or kingdoms in conflict, but fundamentally we find the source of this dilemma to be rooted in our very souls as men.

We are not at peace within ourselves and for good reason. I think it was C.S. Lewis who first described man as a glorious ruin, reflecting upon Adam's fall in Eden and the subsequent effects this had upon all of God's creation. He was describing the marring effect sin has had, defacing the image of God in man. The effects of Adam's fall were indeed catastrophic, crippling our souls, leaving men with abusive, macho ideas about how to lead our wives and children without any real regard for their welfare. Sin is no small thing; it must never be ignored or something we become casual about. Men must remember this.

So, the two burdens a man carries in his soul can be described positively as two special challenges. Yes, we have all fallen in Adam, but the redeemed man has risen with Christ by the gift a free grace; he must now respond, assuming responsibility to chart his future, leaving a meaningful legacy for those who follow. The first of a man's challenges is also his greatest charge: To Remember! The masculine Adam must remember God's commands and be ready to recount the great biblical themes and stories about God. Adam failed to remember and recount God's commandment to his wife while in the Garden of Eden and as a result he partook of the forbidden fruit offered him by Eve. The results of our parent's failure to trust and obey God was and continues to be calamitous for all creation because the lasting effects of their willful decision are as noticeable today as any era in human history.

The second challenge men experience is the Agony of Weightlessness. Do I have what it takes as a redeemed man to enter the chaos of life, bringing order and meaning to my environment along with the ability to shape the things of my domain, making them whole, adding beauty? Men are often plagued with a fear of exposure – being found to be a fraud.

It is true many of us live behind masks, presenting to others our false selves, hoping to conceal our vulnerable selves from criticism. An authentic man on the other hand is not afraid of exposure. He is sure of his identity and purpose, unafraid of shifting opinions of others, and willing to open his private world to persons worthy of trust. So, on that note we will launch from here as males on a journey to manhood. Let's first get an idea of where we're at. How did we get to the place we find ourselves today? We can only answer that question by telling our stories.

MY STORY

Elie Wiesel wrote, "God created man because he loves stories." Again in the movie, <u>Good Will Hunting</u>, therapist Robin Williams tells the troubled Matt Damon something like, "I don't want to read your books or something someone else has said. Tell me about you and I'm fascinated – I'm all in!" Why are we fascinated with the stories of fellow human beings? I think it is because our lives put God on display in ways we cannot otherwise imagine. We examine the lines in a man's face etched and weathered through years of joy and sadness, victory and defeat; these are vestiges of God's fingerprints; we notice all the features, gestures, and voice set forth in the bends and turns of a person's *story*, all the personal experiences being retold of failure and redemption of God's people. Just read the biographical material of men like John Newton or Brennan Manning who tells on himself so repeatedly. We read to see the face of God and dare to believe he could love a wretch like me.

I have often wished I could erase my past. Before I embraced the scandal of the Cross, I cringed when an awful memory of my delinquent past filled my heart with thoughts of reproach and self-contempt, making me reprehensible to myself, alienated from others and feeling alone. The cross has taught me that my sins and abuses of the past required all the verbal abuse and spit, and every stripe, slap, thorn, and nail experienced by Jesus for me. I did not and cannot add an iota of personal merit to the shed blood of Christ on the cross. To think otherwise is to avoid the scandal of the Cross. In addition, Manning writes, "In a futile attempt to erase our past, we deprive the community of our healing gift. If we conceal our wounds out of fear and shame, our inner darkness can neither be illuminated nor become a light to others."

My home of origin was marked by Shame, Fear, Scarcity and Loneliness. I sprung from a family of nine, second oldest in a series of children that are nearly stair-stepped in terms of our birth deliveries which were between 12 and 18 months apart with the exception of my youngest brother who came along unexpectedly after the rest of us were out the door and pretty much on our own.

My father was fresh back home from the Korean War in 1953. In hindsight it is now obvious he carried all the marks of a soul suffering from PTSD. Instead of seeking help he grabbed a bottle in one hand and a carpenter's hammer in the other, forging through life, family in tow, changing residences, more than a dozen times, even moving from state to state. There was never enough to eat. My wife smiles at me to this day; while shopping she often asks, "Do you always have to buy two of everything?" My father was physically and verbally abusive, having no ability to care for himself or the needs of his family. As a result, I stumbled through high school an absolute sot; I joined the Marines at seventeen years of age and headed off to Parris Island in 1973. Following boot camp, I made my way to San Diego for Advanced Infantry Training and then Quantico, VA where grunts like myself engaged Marine officer candidates in warfare in the woods surrounding The Basic School as part of their military training.

While at Quantico I received a meritorious promotion to lance corporal and was so proud of the stripe that I hitchhiked home to the central Midwest to show off my uniform before my mom and dad. Moments after I entered the door of our home, while still standing in the foyer describing my new rank to my mom, my dad appeared and said humorously, "You wouldn't make a pimple on a PFC's ass." This phrase stung me to the core, but I somehow smiled and pretended it had no affect. Johnny Cash's father portrayed in the movie, Walk the Line, pretty much epitomized my dad's behavior, always seeking targets in order to hopelessly shed another layer of personal contempt. Miraculously, my dad came to know Jesus Christ before succumbing to lung cancer. He was a different man before he was placed in the grave and for this I am eternally grateful.

Let me now state the obvious: Each of our lives have a beginning, some kind of formation, stemming from our memory, conscious feelings of inferiority mixed with subconscious choices of superiority, compensations, vows, opinions, and responses to private and public events which taken together becomes a significant point of internal reference as we seek to navigate our future. We each have a story. We are in fact a story, and I can say with confidence that our past is HIS_STORY. God is up to something for you. Are you able to describe your story and understand its current affects upon your life's trajectory? Right now would be a good time to find out where you perceive yourself to be on life's stage, so let's get oriented, using a little map and compass. Following is a graphic that will serve to guide us. Please imagine arrows oriented, pointing downward on the left side of the graphic and arrows oriented, pointing upwards on the right side of the page. Imagine an upside down bell curve with a chasm filling the middle, separating the two sides; let the chasm represent risks and the unknown.

After a bit of reflection where would you say you stand in relation to the swamp and what do you perceive to be your heading? All of us know how many clicks south the swamp lay in relation to our own front door – my personal life map. The question becomes: Have I made up my mind in advance to steer clear of the slough? Some of us are rather casual in response to the question, believing we can flirt with moccasins and not get bit. Others are perhaps lackadaisical, yawning at the prospect of a little immoral dirt beneath my fingernails. But to become vigilant in character; now that person owns a quality we must all seek to carry in our wallet so to speak.

A Road to Manhood Diagram

Where am I Exactly? ///// Becoming a Man

Travel Hazards [Chasm] Wow – Getting Traction

Too Difficult ///// Hey, I Think I Can

Slippery Slope ///// Shattered but not Scattered

* *

SWAMP - - Place of Forgetfulness
Drugs/Alcohol/Pornography/Abuse/Despondency
Pride/Greed/Exploitation/Injustice/Superiority

WHERE AM I EXACTLY?

It's time to name my intersection. This will be an exercise in discovery. In order to find my location on a map I must produce a compass, orient my map north and shoot two azimuths at prominent terrain features, paying attention to the intersection of the back azimuths which will indicate my location. Modern GPS Systems simplify this exercise, but we're in uncharted bush country without smart phones, so a compass is an indispensable piece of gear.

Shooting azimuths on an imaginary "manhood" map might include, bumping into another man whose character impresses you, looking into the mirror and becoming inquisitive about one's own soul, reading spiritual books especially the Bible which provides us with the life description of a Man who is matchless in wisdom, honor, and courage, bearing all manner of kingly qualities due to his singular right to lordship, Jesus Christ, God over all, for sure!

With these resources in hand as well as our mind's eye, we can begin to feel the terrain, mediating on past decisions, successes and failures, asking tough questions like: How do others experience me? Do I have what it takes? Am I able to take my place in community, contributing meaningfully with my time, talents and treasures. Do I feel secure with both of my feet on the ground? Do I belong here on the planet? Am I integrated internally in body, mind, soul and spirit or do I struggle to pull myself together moment by moment due to past wounds or current patterns of sin, leaving me emotionally splintered about my life's purpose, always doubting my value to God. Finally, am I compiling knowledge, applying what I learn, becoming purposeful about my life's direction? Men do life on purpose. They make up their minds about destinations, then tuck away the compass and begin walking the line.

Men from the ranks of blue and white collar labor, impoverished and wealthy, skilled and unskilled alike struggle with the same doubts about their maturity and sense of being grounded. I think it is those men who find their footing (confidence in God), no matter their circumstances, who rise up, move forward, and make a difference in the lives of people around them. Consider for instance the backgrounds and apparent successes of both Senator J.D. Vance and Donald Trump Jr., for although the two men experienced radically different upbringings, both of them emerged as highly respected leaders in their realm of influence, and now as I write, find themselves serving together for the benefit of a much larger whole amidst the GOP. This comparison was recently brought to my attention and I'm sure we could find examples of men of the democratic leadership with similar stories by comparison. I offer this simply as an example of two men from very different origins, men who found their footing and moved forward, making a difference in people's lives. I do not know either of these men personally and therefore know nothing of their motives or moral caliber. Furthermore, we can find these same comparisons being made of men from all kinds of social demographics and backgrounds, not just the political, which sadly has become the focus of so much of our attention here in the United States.

Do you find the violent rhetoric and regular character mauling of opponents by persons of all the political parties represented here in the United States to be utterly appalling and unbecoming? Yes, it is faithfully stirred by a biased media on either side, but we can all turn off the static and remedy our attitudes toward one another by casting our first vote for Christ, following Him as He seeks to bring the Kingdom of God to earth. We must remember that Jesus as well as a scarce few men like Dr. Martin Luther King Jr., John Perkins and a few others sought justice for the downcast without the political assistance from those in seats of power during their lifetimes. It occurs to me, Dr. King may have been assisted later on, but only after much innocent blood had been spilled and it was becoming politically advantageous for persons with political careers to get on board the Peace Movement for social justice. I am reminded of the old cliché, "Talk is cheap." No matter if I'm a plumber, politician, preacher or painter, I must always strive to say what I mean, mean what I say, and *do* what I say. Our deeds validate our words, and great leaders have shown us action always beats policy.

Let's move on. So, what if I'm rejected or scorned by others? Do I know how to get up and move forward without bearing the weight of resentment or vengefulness, weights that must be carefully considered and then discarded, for it is always wise to travel light in this world?

Pretty soon we find our spot on the map. We lace up our shoes and figure out a path forward, because life and responsibilities call us to the pavement as men whether we like it or not. For this reason, we must make regular inventory of our private world, laying our internal parts bare before God and trustworthy friends. Just as a compass needs to be calibrated before use, we ourselves need daily re-calibration before entering the challenges of our world. Brennan Manning writes, "Silent solitude makes true speech possible and personal. If I am not in touch with being beloved, then I cannot touch the sacredness of others. If I am estranged from myself, I am likewise a stranger to others." Beginning each day in *quiet time* with God, reading and meditating on His Word is assuredly the single most soul strengthening practice I have ever committed to in terms of investment of time vis a vis spiritual reward.

I think most young men begin right here a little bewildered, but confident too with enough personal skill and testosterone to propel them to the next level. They pass through puberty, they observe other men working, playing, and relating. After some trial and error they understand their own likes and dislikes and begin feeling comfortable in their own skin as it were; they begin feeling as though they too can provide for themselves and make a unique contribution, impacting others in positive ways.

As early as middle-school, young men are often invited into the trades alongside their fathers, laying brick, plumbing homes, raising framed walls or else gaining exposure to white collar work such as accounting, engineering, and a long list of other professional opportunities. The point is young men at an early age observe, dream, then roll up their sleeves and begin getting their hands dirty in the various soils of life. This is all well and good and even predictable.

Fast-forward a few years and a man might find himself, kicking back in his first stuffed recliner with a cold beverage in hand, watching his favorite NFL team crush the visitors. He whispers to himself during commercial break, "Ah, life is good. I found a wife, enjoy my work, earn a good wage, have good friends and find ways to recreate or devote time to hobbies. The road before me feels level with a good line of sight. I've got great intuition and besides I'm fully insured against all manner of road hazards."

The man in the chair deserves the comfy cushions and a day off from work because he has earned it. He's cut his piece of the American pie and savoring every bite. And even with the rise of the Millennial and Alpha generations, young and old alike will continue aspiring to some form of the American Dream; however some predict that sprouting generations will grow increasingly apathetic, entitled, and non-committed to anything but self, due to declining morale, lack of opportunity compared with previous generations, and the ever increasing burden of social media. But even this posture, so opposite say to the Boomers, it will still characterize the majority population of that future generation and should therefore be carefully considered.

With the birth of the smart phone in recent decades and quickly emerging AI, Generation Alpha will see their dream come true, creating perhaps a very different American than who I am and those I've been relating to all my life. Will there still be male human beings born to future generations? Will these young men need navigational assistance, charting paths in an over grown environment? Yes. Culture will change, and new generations will follow Alpha if the world survives, and there will always be need for the old guard to call forth the masculine seed placed in the core of a man, nourishing it and making it grow. I believe men will be available in that day to sow, cultivate, and reap a crop of leaders in whatever the environment for the survival of the species and the great glory of man's Maker. Generations can deteriorate and they can also be made better so long as a few men stay on the alert and act like men.

TRAVEL HAZARDS

Have you ever hit an obstacle figuratively or literally while trying to move from one place to the next? You envisioned a clear path with your wife at your side, perhaps "running down a dream" as Tom Petty once sang. Let me interrupt those lyrics with a closed railroad crossing, a bridge collapse, a car pile-up, tree over the road or a host of other obstacles we hadn't counted on. Life now begins to mock us – you can't get there from here – you're weak and incompetent – you fool; why did you ever leave the comforts of home?

I was in the middle of graduate school when my dear wife experienced an emotional collapse that brought our lives to a standstill for many months; and although I completed my degree, her needs and my commitment to her well-being changed the course of our lives. I was far from being a developed confident man in those early years and the fear about our future was begging me to somehow return to my boyhood. A boy can wait out a train delay, a boy can grab a chain saw and remove a tree from the road, but a boy cannot mend the soul of his spouse; this will require seeing her face to face and entering her agony as a man, something I was in no way prepared for as an underdeveloped thirty-year-old.

This was not a fender bender. My wife's sudden breakdown felt like a head on collision, requiring triage of passengers in both front and rear seats. I remember saying to myself, *it's over. How do I gracefully clean up this mess, pull everything into my control, back away from school and slip away quietly without too much exposure? I need to get my wife and family "off grid," where I can further assess the damage and figure out a way forward.* My own personal unprocessed shame clouded my senses, limiting my ability to remember a single promise from God.

I had limited ability in the early years of my marriage to speak into chaos and evoke change, little ability to assure my wife the wreck wasn't her fault and I had a plan that would serve to steer us back on track.

Could I remember God? By his grace and the assistance of some unusually compassionate members of our church we were able to tow our wrecked lives to safety, and resume travel over the road some months later. I wish I had the awareness at this time how much I needed another man in my life who had walked this road before. My wife suffered much neglect because I didn't have the wisdom to repair her heart.

Relationship strengthening tools were not offered me as a young person. In fact life skills in relational training for young adults entering marriage was nearly unheard of in my experience, growing up in the 70's. There were no pre-conditions for marriage save your blood types being compatible – no driver's training or series of multiple choice questions to test one's comprehension. All tests, pass or fail, occurred right out on the boulevards of life.

Observing my marriage through the rearview mirror, I felt my gift of service was adequate, lifting burdens and household chores, but my wife and I limped along for several more years due to my inability to come all the way around and meet her face to face as a woman, caring for her emotional needs. I was largely ignorant and unable to perceive the strengths, but also the needs of her feminine soul. But looking back, I must smile at God's wisdom and also quiver before His tender mercies when I realize he towed two jalopies to His chop shop, one an off road four-wheeler with great power and durability the other a light weight convertible with wonderful versatility. The Master Craftsman joined these two makes and together they became capable of some serious endurance runs such as we see during the Baja 500.

Other "Calls to Duty," have been presented to me throughout life. I've since discovered that I don't have to be a polished orator to resolve problems, but I do have to find my voice as a man and speak up on behalf of my wife, family, community and for justice all around.

When your daughter brings her broken heart to you, looking for advice; this is no time to grab a beer and slip off to the garage and sort tools. She needs her dad. Being a man isn't about the outward but the inward parts of a man's soul. The apostle Paul smiled at his critics' assessment of himself. They said his personal appearance is unimpressive and his speech contemptible. Paul may not have had any abs or significant stature, but his heart was on full-tilt for God and that commitment is what made him great.

Whatever the road hazard we encounter in life, the choice must be made to trust God's goodness and walk through the difficulty by faith or else forget about God's story and muscle through life, creating outcomes only I can control. The prophet Isaiah warns all of us to beware and not "light our own fires" when catastrophe strikes and doubts arise, for to those who light their own fires the prophet warns, "You will lie down in torment." God loves the soul who follows him during periods of darkness, trusting his goodness and faithful provision.

I've briefly described a single incident above that nearly wiped me out. Imagine the life of the Patriarch Jacob and the number of obstacles he encountered in life. The man did double the labor for what was promised him because his employer deceived him. He quit his job and moved his family a great distance only to run right into the face of his estranged brother he figured was out to kill him. Jacob handled these obstacles, losing loved ones along the way, including his wife, Rachael, who died delivering Jacob's twelfth son. Jacob wrestled with God in a very literal sense, finally found pasture for his flocks and began to settle into community when his daughter was raped and his sons retaliated with fierce recompense, slaughtering the enemy's entire camp. Jacob lost his favored son presumably to a wild beast; he faced famine, forcing him to move yet again to an unknown territory. He one day declared before Pharaoh, King of Egypt, "I haven't lived as long as my fathers, in fact, my days have been few and evil upon the earth."

Jacob faced some serious road hazards on his road to manhood, including an encounter with God which left him limping along on a crutch, but as far as I can tell he never cowered from his responsibilities as a man. While in route, he commanded his family put away their idols;

he was a spiritual guide besides offering intercession and ruling his clan as a king, offering them direction, protection and provision for their vulnerable lives – people who were counting on him to remember his God.

From here we return to our own personal stories, looking to the next horizon; we will encounter a world that glitters, calling for our attention. So, the world has its own call, but we must remember God's call. The woman, Folly calls from all corners of the market place, urging the naïve to turn in to her residence and drink stolen water in secret places. Wisdom on the other hand has built her house and spread her table with aged wine and choice meats reserved for nobility – those who eat for strength, not drunkenness. The high road is not always the easiest road, and I've found the *narrow gate* has often squeezed me in ways I would never be touched out amidst the broad concourse of life. Always remember that whatever difficulties you endure in this life are but momentary light afflictions and not worth comparing to the glories yet to be revealed to those who overcome. The Lord Jesus remarks again and again as recorded in the Apostle John's account of the Revelation given him: He who overcomes will be rewarded, granted access, given a new name as well as many other priceless bestowments from God. In the end, count road hazards as opportunities to get to know God better.

TOO DIFFICULT

During the first week of training on Parris Island, the drill instructor marched our platoon over to the battalion parade deck, allowing us to watch a graduation ceremony – third phase recruits who had passed the tests of training in the blood, sweat and tears of a very hot and humid South Carolina coast. He wanted to instill in us the vision that whatever lay before us could be conquered and that we too would one day graduate and move on from boot camp to duty among the fleet Marine Corps.

Every man will be faced with obstacles and difficulties throughout life, hazards as we mentioned before, blocking the road, creating stressors that feel overwhelming at times. Responsible men carry significant burdens upon their shoulders. Besides providing for their families, men take their place in faith, civic or other cultural communities committed to improving the quality of life on every hand; their everyday habits of participation in this world becomes the crucible for personal refinement and the "test of their metal." Yes, life is very tough at times, but we must never lose sight of our graduation day as men.

Moving along life's road to manhood, subtle but felt mocking's can sometimes be heard cutting at our confidence, challenging everything we have come to believe about God's story and his undying commitment to us. A mother might forget her child, but God has promised to never lose sight of us. How easily we forget, and there, right there begins the doubts, bad decisions, defamation and pending derailment; there is perhaps nothing more emotionally debilitating than submitting to the voice of one's false self, running loose on the interior of one's soul with a megaphone, shouting reproach for our failures. Let it be said, "God is O.K. with failure so long as we get back up." There is no shame in failure, quite the contrary, for failure demonstrates you took your best shot with a faulty gun handed you, getting back up says you're willing to aim again, adjusting for wind and elevation.

Those who refuse to get back up begin dreaming about what life might be "over there." Let me now introduce the chasm that separates us from where we're at and over there. Please refer to the graphic up above – the deep bowl with tall sides. At various points in our journeys as men we imagine a better world with fewer obstacles or at least a world in which I am conquering obstacles without too much trouble, moving forward in terms of life goals. Any such pursuit of success will require a measure of risk, launching into the unknown. There is an invisible chasm that separates us from our present reality and that which we envision of our future – our hope.

Reaching that destination is costly; becoming a man will require courage and strength, and most importantly personal faith in God. Setting our eyes on a distant land doesn't transport us there except in one's dreams. Also, travelling a road free of obstacles does not exist over there either. The *Over There* is not a problem free land of fairies and free dairy. No, because a topographical map will reveal to us hills, valleys, canyons and mountain tops with roads very much like the ones we're now traversing; however, these passages become decisive paths that energizes us with each step as we place one foot before the other and prayerfully proceed with a strong sense of purpose. It is exhilarating to *walk* in God's world as a man just as it is for a woman to *walk* as a woman – image bearers whose souls pulse with unique gender defining qualities, matching who they are – their purpose, style and role in a world created by God for our joy and His good pleasure.

When life becomes too difficult we have the opportunity to capitulate, turn around or veer off the path entirely. Some of the obstacles men deem indomitable include: Betrayal, Cowardice and Ambivalence. These are enemies of a man's soul and will require courage and inner resolve to put them down. One's inability or unwillingness to confront enemies with confidence and strength will render a man powerless, assigned to slavery.

Betrayal is an especially nasty wound and those who have been struck by this club have felt its weight and been slow to get back on their feet. Betrayal leaves the soul of its target bleeding out trust, bewildered about direction often losing the will to fight. Have you ever been delivered into the hands of your enemies by a trusted friend? King David tells us the story of such an experience, explaining that his good friend, with whom he once enjoyed meals and good fellowship, lifted up his "heel," against him. The betrayal was unexpected. We assume David enjoyed spending time with this person, sharing secrets and many personal stories, only to be turned against and exposed to others in some shameful way.

I have known the feeling of betrayal and it was devastating to my soul. After I had been used by a friend, helping him ascend ladders to success, he turned on me, denying he ever knew me. I'm describing a man I had come to trust and share intimate details about my personal life and marriage. I was no longer considered part of this person's affiliation of friends, rather that of an outlying loathsome caste of which he could no longer associate. I later discovered this man also had immoral designs for my wife and other women of our fellowship, masquerading as a therapist.

The entire experience with this person was utterly appalling in hindsight. I was left feeling like a complete fool, but this person's deceptive skills were rivaled only by such as the Devil himself – evil masquerading as an angel of light so "sacred" were his verses and lies. This experience awakened me to the power of deceit, like a big splash of water in my face, letting me know first-hand there's no reward for the naïve. This experience wounded my soul, but of course also made me wiser, reminding me of the cliché, "Once burned twice learned." Jesus suffered the ultimate betrayal by his friend, Judas. Jesus was a man of immense courage; He showed us that even a blow this severe can be endured if we keep our eyes on God. For example, please notice how Jesus continued serving His disciples after He knew full well the betrayal had begun, leading to His crucifixion.

Another monster in a young man's path is the enemy of Cowardice. Did you know if you call a woman a coward she is likely to brush it off and even turn and offer you a slice of pie with a fresh poured cup of your favorite coffee? A woman's soul is not designed like a man's soul. She doesn't feel *coward* the same way a man does. Now, if you call a woman a whore, she is likely to slap you across the face and challenge you to a duel. Whether coward or whore, an individual's response will depend entirely upon their gender which is God-given and it's deeply engrained – a very definite identity marker placed inside by Him, making men and women unique image bearers of God.

So, call a man, any size man a coward – touch your pistols – and see what happens! When a man is called a coward he will get up from his place and meet his opponent eye to eye as long as he is nearly the same size and weight, for a man also knows, "when to hold them and when it's time to fold them." A man can bear many burdens, but he cannot bear the burden of being considered a coward. Someone once said a sure cure for alcoholism is for the alcoholic to stand before a mirror and repeatedly confess that he is an alcoholic, i.e. a coward. This simple exercise will often sober up a man and place him back on the road to manhood. I think the founders of A.A. may have made this discovery early on because they invite all members to identify themselves as being an alcoholic before they speak into the mic and begin relating their personal stories.

Lastly, there is the enemy of Ambivalence. This is the subtle sinister one, urging us to not get too excited, there will always be tomorrow, relax and rethink your options, then further relax and rethink until the time is past and everything begins to lock-up on the inside due to disuse; and we find ourselves in utter apathy with no motivation to defend our ground nor move forward to new heights. Ambivalence is an internal cry of surrender. Leave me alone. I have no opinion. Let my wife handle it! The ambivalent man feels weightless because he's shed his garments of glory; he brings nothing to the table and appears before God with empty hands. Throughout the history of Israel, all males were to appear before God three times per year and they dare not show up empty-handed. The Apostle Paul also urges us in one of his epistles to stand up and act like men.

These are formidable enemies and I have encountered them all, each more than once in life and I did not always perform in the most admirable fashion. God wants us to fight for our souls and the souls of our loved ones. When the road to manhood feels most difficult, when the chasm feels too risky, too wide and the other side far out of reach – this is the time to solicit the help of others, collaborating with other men, choosing not to remain in isolation, but to step up and confess my need for genuine community – a band of brothers who can help in times of need. Set-up a stronghold with like-minded men who share your faith in the risen Christ; tell your stories to one another, understand one another's battle scars, tell of your victories as well as your defeats. Nothing bonds men more permanently than telling, hearing and receiving stories from one another, answering the questions: where are you from and where are you going, and who are you really? Men who cower from their responsibilities and life's calling as a man find themselves on the leading edge of a very slippery slope, veering off the road into unauthorized territory.

SLIPPERY SLOPE

I want to be a boy again. I don't want to grow up and assume the responsibilities of an adult male, becoming a man. I don't want to bear the mantle of leadership for friends and spouse and children if married. What a difference leaders make in whatever realm they find themselves. I'm reminded of a line from the Song of Deborah and Barak found in the first verse of the Book of Judges, chapter five which reads, "That the leaders led in Israel!" And because the leaders led, Israel was able to defeat Sisera and his armies which boasted nine hundred iron chariots. The victors of Israel during this period burst into song when they observed the power and effect of applied leadership. I think we all recognize nations drift without proper leadership as do families, and so do individuals who fail to exercise proper self-government.

The slippery slope is the path of a fool who has discarded his moral compass. He believes life will always require too much fortitude and endurance from him, deciding therefore to make the most of his time while on earth, seldom considering an eternal state which will follow this present temporal state of being.

A fool is not a man. The fool described in Scripture is not simply a silly comic, rather a dangerous immoral person who should not be counted upon to come through for you. Indeed, a fool should be avoided at all costs for Solomon warns, bumping into one at the wrong time can be as frightful as meeting a sow bear robbed of her cubs.

The slippery slope has seen many young men pass through her hands to the abyss below; young men unwilling to fight for their souls, unwilling to seek the safety of brotherhood among trustworthy friends. As Proverbs again warns: He who separates himself seeks his own desire, he quarrels against all sound wisdom. The coward ignores all this, choosing instead to claw around slick clay banks scarcely avoiding the swamp below his feet. After all, they've watched Tom Cruise dangle with one hand from cliffs and high speed trains only to arrive safely time and again at a prescribed destination with both of his feet on the ground.

Men learn early on to dispense with illusory thoughts about their own strength and capabilities. They are persons of sound understanding and able to separate faith from fantasy, my home address and activities from stories that fill the pages of fiction novels. Men know their own capacities and limitations because they have been tested and have grown to understand who it is God has made them to be. And this understanding brings contentment because it rests upon the foundation of trust a man has with his Maker. We believe His wise design and thank Him for the bestowment of gifts given to us by Him.

So, how do we call young men enamored with the wrong kind of risks and adventures away from the slippery slope? Besides being adventurous many young persons live with a strong sense of immortality: What foul thing could possibly happen to me? This is not an easy task, serving as negotiator, reasoning with a person held hostage by his own lusts. They tell us, "I know it's not healthy, I agree it's not moral, I know I'll regret this, but, but, but ..."

Let's face it, there is so much allure in culture, calling youth to dimly lit backstreets and the gutters of cities as well as sketchy taverns and honky-tonks galore, providing city born and rural alike plenty of opportunity to play. Is there an exit ramp available for young men caught up in a circle of despair always looking for cheap thrills to satisfy their thirsty souls only to be left broken down and forsaken at the side of the road when the party's over?

Friend, there is right now, has always been, and will forever be a bridge right here at this dangerous juncture, offering us safe passage to the other side of the abyss and onto the bank facing north. The signage is clear and has been featured all along the road to manhood. Jesus welcomes struggling sojourners to take his hand, allowing him to pull them from slippery slopes to safety. Unfortunately, foolish boys are reluctant to grow up and as mentioned above often finding themselves playing in dangerous territories, anonymous among men, just looking for another good time while squandering their wealth and soiling their reputations with cheap offers – scrap pleasures of this present darkness.

THE SWAMP

We are capable of making a ruin of our lives. Afterwards, some bow down in failure, staring at problems, cradling their face in both palms, feeling they've hit rock bottom. I must ask this person to relax. The real problem is much worse. The prophet Jeremiah tells us, "The heart is more deceitful than all else and desperately sick; who can understand it?" You see, it will do no good to tinker with repairs; the heart must be yanked out and replaced. Keep reading and see if you will agree.

The swamp on our graph represents a place of utter forgetfulness. Cowards, those with self-inflicted wounds, and the naïve populate this stagnant slough, men who found life's call to be too difficult are found in this swamp, ankle deep, waist deep or fully submerged they're all here, avoiding responsibilities while many claiming to be the very epitome of a man due to the size of their biceps or private parts they bow down to as their god. Images of some of these parts are sometimes displayed, dangling on the trailer hitch of their oversized 4 X 4 pick-up trucks that have never been driven a mile off a paved road. I'm not being sarcastic or cruel. I feel sorrow in my heart as I pen these words, realizing how I once shared the road with these boys as a young man myself, swimming in the same swamp, croaking out my gripes to God, never understanding how my own folly was ruining my life.

How can a prodigal so marred with filth and shame ever hope to crawl out of the swamp and dry off? All the emptiness, loss, slop and starvation for life makes one cry out in earnestness – in gut wrenching pain, saying, "I want to go home." The path home begins with a breath of aspiration. We look up from the muck and discover a sky overhead and muse about a world beyond. The squanderer of sacred treasure catches a glimpse of God even in the swamp; he remembers life back on Dad's farm and wonders if he might be accepted if he returns home.

This is where miracles occur. Lyrics from the song, *Show Me Your Glory* by Third Day include: I caught a glimpse of Your splendor / In the corner of my eye / The most beautiful thing I've ever seen / And it was like a flash of lightning / Reflected off the sky / And I know I'll never be the same. A revelation from God can break through from heaven at any moment. We awake to a new song. We awake to the realization that God is a Father awaiting his child's return home. Divine love, when received by prodigals always results in hope. Our desire does not change us. The kindness of God changes us – His goodness is the spark that sets our new hearts aflame.

Image bearers were not designed to swim in a swamp. Man was not created for himself alone; he was created to exalt his Creator in thought, word and deed and to walk with him in fellowship, performing redemptive works in the midst of a fallen world.

Listen to how the prophet speaks of the heart of Christ saying, "A bruised reed I will not break and a smoldering wick I will not quench." We might say Jesus stood waist deep in the middle of a great swamp at Calvary, holding up a bridge for any who call upon him in truth, anyone seeking rescue. God will hear the cry of a man drowning in sin, for He is infinite in kindness and mighty to save. In the midst of the swamp, Jesus raises above his head the cross upon which he hung when he gave up his life for the sins of the world. This costly bridge provides a wide beam – a walking surface to step up from the swamp and run to the far bank for safety and a moment of rest.

All of us naturally long for relief in a world of monotony, a world often filled with disappointment and shattered dreams. Unfortunately opportunities offered in the environs of the swamp, though temporarily satisfying, never bring the pure and lasting joy gained by those participating in activities that are conducted in the full light of day.

I think the men who step up from the swamp are men who come to the stark realization that my life experience is not working for me. I keep returning to the same dead end with the same hands full of disappointments. A crevice opens in the back of my throat and I cry for a power greater than me to lift me from the shambles and remove all the stains. I don't want to die like this. There is still time. I have had plenty of energy to play in the wrong places, I will have energy to labor joyfully in an invisible kingdom which promises delight mixed with persecutions, temporal satisfaction with delayed gratification made complete in heaven. I want to live for a greater purpose. I want to put away my selfish pleasures and begin to put God on display in my everyday life.

SHATTERED BUT NOT SCATTERED

"The stone which the builders rejected, this became the chief cornerstone. Everyone who falls on this stone will be broken to pieces, but upon whomever it falls, it will scatter him like dust." [Matthew 21:44] Drought, hunger and misery make for a powerful vice, delivering pain, bringing one to his senses. We begin to remember again. The prodigal brings the past into the present, remembering what life was like before he left the safety of the farm. Brennan Manning writes somewhere to the effect: We come to grips with our own selfishness and stupidity, we make friends with the imposter and accept that we are impoverished and broken and realize if we were not, we would be God. Manning offers further guidance saying, we must be gentle with ourselves which becomes our gentleness with others.

I know of no one who tests the elasticity of the gospel quite like Brennan Manning. People who have been broken, as Brennan often confesses of himself, simply write and behave differently than others. No matter the soiled condition of a human soul, wasting away in the bottom of a swamp, being filled with drugs, pornography, alcohol abuse, pride and all the rest; Manning insists as does the gospel of Isaiah: God will not break a bruised reed not snuff out a dimply burning wick. The grace of our Lord Jesus Christ is more marvelous than we can possibly imagine or find words to properly explain. We are shattered internally at the prospect of free grace and complete reinstatement, but not scattered as chaff in the wind – these are the faithless who ignore or despise such amazing grace.

Grace is not an elevator ride to the top. Anyone drying out on the bank, having been snatched from the swamp and walking the cross beam to safety can tell you so. These men just like the ones who chose higher ground early on must continue solving problems, face difficulties and make tough decisions that will always require personal involvement of their souls. Men must remember God's story. Men meditate upon God's word; reflect upon their own life experiences, bringing meaning and purpose to their walk with God. Change begins with a single breath of aspiration, and continues to be fueled by remembering him, relying upon him in everything. The wisest of God's representatives displayed in the Bible were persons who clung to God. This is a picture of dependency that must be discovered by one battered soul at a time. We discover that God is always good no matter my circumstances or present life experiences. The Evil One thinks differently about this always looking for opportunities to pull a man into denial or betrayal of God. So, remember God, recount his faithfulness, develop your new heart, thanking Him for his lovingkindness which is everlasting as the Psalmist confirms repeatedly.

HEY, I THINK I CAN

To remember is to obey. We begin to dream again. Wisdom overcomes folly; foolishness is replaced with reverence for the Lord. We perform the deeds we did at first, lest Jesus come and take away our candlestick. God will give you the means to get home. Looking back briefly at the swamp, a man coming to his senses can now laugh, shed tears and perhaps laugh again at how utterly stupid addictions are in every form. No man would ever consider walking around publicly or privately sucking on his thumb until it resembled a prune.

Of course this is laughable, but tragically is precisely the very form and function of addictions. Boys long for the comfort of mother and if not properly weaned will satisfy this felt need in the form of a bottle of booze, weed or a host of other things one craves in excess, pampering the flesh, taking care of *Number One*.

Men on the other hand move away from a desire for milk and grow in their appetite for meat. It should be pointed out women in general and mothers in particular embody a strength camouflaged before the eyes of boys. This is one of the chief reasons boys turn to pornography and the abuse of women – they are afraid to stand face to face with a woman, but they don't know why. If they happen to be married to a strong woman they will shrink back entirely because a man must assuredly be a man if he ever hopes to be with a woman of strength.

These days pornography – nakedness – is readily available in so many forms – digitally displayed in ways we never thought possible; it becomes so cheap and familiar it loses any sense of beauty, being made common and made to compare with the next nude body one sees. A boy at work commented the other day saying, "If you've seen one set of breasts, you've got to see them all!" He chuckled and rolled along about his work never understanding his own personal slavery for he often spoke of his sexual exploits and male prowess among women. Little does he know that regular, ongoing graphic exposure to female genitals as well as videos featuring intercourse in every way imaginable, leads to perversion in a man's soul, wreaking havoc with his internal senses, while making peace with enemies that will most assuredly destroy his soul, marriage and heritage if not combatted. On the other hand, men who love their wives and dutifully protect their marriages from foreign enemies are some of the first to laugh at this ridiculous addiction – slavery to pornography, for they understand the cowardice that lies beneath the acts of an addict, coaching him to remain safely anonymous not too far from mother's arms.

Apart from the gift of repentance, these males will never know the experience of proper attachment between a man and woman who mate for life as beautiful swans. They will never experience the amazing connection, the joy, the exhilaration of manhood and womanhood properly celebrated by simply looking into one another's eyes, sharing the things we together name, and experiencing sex as God intended, fresh springs no one else is permitted to touch.

Boy's must get beyond mother's protection if they ever hope to become a man, and pornography is simply a laughable example of how boys cling to a perverted image of conquering *the her* in some odd manner, leaving them altogether impotent to enter or penetrate their world in any reproductive, meaningful sense. Robert Bly speaks about this dilemma in his book, <u>Iron John</u>. Using the form of riddle he tells his readers, "A young man must slip the key from beneath mother's pillow, being aware she is a light sleeper."

Real change is possible. You do not have to remain chained to a destructive addiction. The best way to break an addictive habit is to simply join other men on the road to manhood, men very much like yourself with similar stories of bondage and freedom, but men nevertheless who risked being known by others. We step into the light, exposing ourselves for who we are, offering others our unadorned selves which is our authentic selves – now real living can begin, for nobody wants to listen to another droning story from the life of a phony showing up simply to be accountable.

Accountability to another man does not require trust in fact it weakens trust; it assumes I'm lying and your job is to uncover the secret self I'm hiding from you. In the end, accountability among men gets pretty confusing and ridiculous. We must begin any relationship by being honest with ourselves and in turn honest with brothers. I must feel the freedom to tell you what's going on in my private world or withhold for reasons perhaps unknown to even me.

There is no need to be, "held accountable." Men who hold one another accountable think they're being spiritual, think they're being a brother's keeper. This philosophy has been tested through various men's movements and found to be a useless exercise in deceit. I used to regularly relate to a man who used the word "accountable" as frequently as my pastor might use a word like grace. This man espoused this conviction without shame all the while being physically involved with a woman outside his marriage who was half his age. It doesn't stop here, for I could fill a book with similar stories of hypocrisy – men trying to be God's sheriff to others while living scandalous private lives hidden from friends. Look, men will relate as men; stories will be told and revelations made as trusting relationships build and bond. These men will then find hope to press on for the improvement of our lives and families. We will leave a lasting mark on another human life and really this is all that can be hoped for – this is the top – when we impart something solid to another human being for Jesus' sake.

In terms of "showing up" in my home and community, we might consider startling our loved ones by adopting words drawn from the movie: The Gladiator, "I will show them something they have never seen before." Glory excites a man. The Hebrew meaning of the word, "Glory," is weight. Every man carries a secret desire in his heart to become a heavy weight, not world conqueror or subduer of others, rather to be felt by family and friends in meaningful ways, including personal care and protection. Every male wants to be regarded as a man, not an adolescent in a 30 or 40 year old body.

Theoretically, this all sounds easy enough, but how does a man respond, arriving home from work, finding his wife distressed, cooking dinner with small children at her apron strings with demands of their own? A man must always be ready and willing to assume leadership, stepping in wherever necessary, lifting burdens and placing his own needs behind the needs of his family. Wise men learn the rhythm of their homes, finding ways to recreate and replenish themselves so as to be available to send Mom to the couch or a bedroom retreat away from the demands of her children for reprieve and quiet moments of rest. Men are alert to the tempo of the home and decide as necessary to evacuate the kids, driving over to the park for play when life's band inside the home gets too loud and unruly.

After slaying the giants, George MacDonald has Anodos, the protagonist in the novel, Fantasties saying, "I learned that it is better, a thousand-fold, for a proud man to fall and be humbled, than to hold up his head in his fancied innocence. I learned that he who would be a hero, will barely be a man; that he will be nothing but a doer of his work, is sure of his manhood." This remark strikes like a hammer on a great bell. Relax and learn not to take yourself too seriously. Simply love well, provide and guide and you will do many natural but wonderful exploits most of which will never occur to you.

WOW, GETTING TRACTION

Faith, hope and love are revived as gifts from a generous Maker who has not forgotten our names. The prodigal comes to his sense through the gift or remembrance, he rises from the swamp by an act of divine grace; he is slammed to a rock lying on a dry bank where he is shattered into pieces, broken and crying aloud to God in hopes of ever being integrated again. The healing comes, one tear at a time, one step at a time, until we step back up on the lawn at Abba's house only to be met with an avalanche of acceptance and gifts we cannot possibly contain. Our chests explode and implode; we lift our heads then fall on our faces before such undeserved love. This love did not originate here on earth, but had to come down in order for us to experience it – the love of God that touches the shoulders of a sin-ravaged child fallen on his knees before him. God shells out many brisk joyful commands: Place my signet ring on his finger, shoes on his feet, wrap him in my robe and slaughter the fattened calf. My child has returned and is now safe and sound.

Friends, let it be said, there is no spiritual requirement for a person to enter the swamp in order to experience redemption as a child of God – not at all. On the other hand, nobody becomes a child of God without first having a devastating personal encounter with the Rock. Every soul will fall upon the Rock and either experience the brokenness displayed by the sinful woman recorded in the seventh chapter of St. Luke's gospel and that of Peter following his denial of the Lord, or else walk away from the offer of free grace and one day see a shadow darken their steps followed by a crashing blow, a huge boulder, slamming them to the earth, leaving them scattered to the four winds. It would be an eternal mistake to ignore God, choosing a life of independence away from the personal, loving fellowship He offers every human being.

Faith hope and love must be exercised like muscles in our arms. We can now dream again. Faith is a spark of trust, creating a glow in our stomachs, lifting our countenance, emanating in our faces. Faith is the assurance of things hoped for. The man of faith doesn't focus on the things that are seen, realizing the things that matter, the things that are unseen, are eternal. Abraham the father of faith was a man who never quite got his garden in. Like him we are strangers here on earth – we keep moving, keeping step with God's Spirit always leaning into the future with prayers and intercessions for ourselves and others. Hope is our compass. Our eyes are on a distant palace whose architect and builder is God. Hope rises even during times of distress and tribulation, when we reflect upon God's impeccable record of faithfulness. Finally, love is the pie we share with our loved ones and indeed the world. It's too sweet to describe, one must taste for himself and see the Lord is good.

Can we envision a life that embodies these jewel-like qualities? Can you imagine a life guided by faith, hope and love with God as your exceeding joy? At a pivotal moment in the movie: <u>The Gladiator</u>, Russell Crowe, offers a former dishonored gladiator redemption by asking him: "Are you in danger of becoming a good man?" This person stood upon the threshold of decision. How do you answer this question?

BECOMING A MAN

Zachar [Hebrew for: Remembering one]. Men experience the best feeling ever when they walk and relate with God as they are designed. Men of God are known in the gates; moreover, men of God serve their families via the tri-fold office of Prophet, Priest and King.

Being a prophet is a state of mind. He knows the truth and protects it from corruption. A prophet must speak up, unmasking pretensions, naming sin and abusive behaviors, calling out cowardice when it surfaces, reminding everyone of that which is written.

A Priest orients his family, calling them to prayer. A priest is an intercessor after the pattern of Jesus. We must strive to always believe and experience the power of prayer. After years of experience, I believe nothing of eternal significance occurs apart from prayer. God is exalted by answering prayer and we experience a taste of his joy when we join him in the process and victory processions!

The king is not afraid to say, "No." He rules well within the bounds of sacred nobility. Like the prophet, the king must also speak. The king is a true heavy weight without any nagging sense of weightlessness for he understands a glory bestowed, operating by commission under the mighty hand of God to whom all glory is due. The King is no despot or abuser of power. He understands his domain and takes great interest in the welfare of his family.

Legacy is of course that which we leave behind for others to consider. How will I be remembered? Did I hand off the baton at the place of rendezvous after completing my lap in the world? At the end of our lives we may be missing a button or two like the Velveteen Rabbit, but we will have the satisfaction we lived well and gave our strength for others, lifting burdens, offering guidance, giving of our emotional and material resources for the wellbeing of my neighbor.

Humility is a secret treasure – a character quality to be acquired then hidden from sight. It opposes pride, which Thomas Merton describes as, "A stubborn insistence on being what we are not and never were intended to be . . . an exorbitant demand that others believe the lie we have made ourselves believe about ourselves."

The closing scene of the movie: <u>The Wizard of Oz</u> is a wonderful dramatization of neurosis in full bloom, and since everyone on the planet suffers at some level with the problem of neurosis we can talk about it openly for a moment. As you remember, Dorothy and her friends enter the Emerald City and approach the fearful OZ in order to make requests of him. The Wizard responds with bellowing smoke and frightening sounds. However, when the curtain is pulled away by Dorothy's dog, we observe a little bald man shouting into a microphone, manipulating levers, announcing his greatness.

The great wizard was suddenly laid bare, with nothing to offer his visitors but his unadorned self. Only then was he able to present his new friends with specific gifts by speaking into them with solid words, creating realizations of truths that were already present, strengths buried beneath possible slander and lies from previous times. Dorothy's friends received words of affirmation and were therefore helped. Neurosis occurs due to an individual's empty pursuit of a fictitious goal of superiority. Like the Great Oz, we live like neurotics, believing we must be great beyond our companions. In reality the neurotic is always seeking it seems to shore up or hide his feelings of inferiority, over compensating, leading to alienation and loneliness behind a curtain of shame. Someone faithful (*a Fido*), must turn back the curtain and tell us the truth. Now everyone can be seen and experience healing. Someone once said, "When a man comes to you and tells you your own story, (e.g. pulls back the curtain) you know that your sins are forgiven. And when you are forgiven, you are healed."

Jesus tells us that we become great when we serve our companions, offering them our unadorned selves, calling out what we know resides inside other image bearers. This is a great calling for every man. When a man sits in solitude and quietness of soul he can nearly hear God's voice at the end of the day saying, "Welcome home. Well done good and faithful servant. You trusted Me."

This booklet was conceived out of personal need, and I confess that I write "above myself." However, we cannot afford to wait and speak until after we have arrived at some state of perceived perfection or attainment of complete wholeness. Rather we must remain prophetic, never lowing the bar, but instead always ready to call one another up to attainable goals on our road to manhood.

I do not have any claims to greatness. Most of my mobility in life has been jagged it seems, up and down, sideways, including detours and long one-way streets when I walked alone. It appears I did not understand my own gifts and calling until the proper time had passed. Much of this was due to some of the things I've written about: detours, cowardice, poor decisions, sabotage and others. I've discovered through it all that I can count upon Jesus, the Author and Finisher of my faith. He has been up to something for my life all along. It has often times looked upside down, but he has always been there for he has promised to never forsake me.

Passages I made in life seldom felt chosen – life happened and I reacted. God knows. In the end I can place my head on my pillow each night, realizing that by the grace of God alone I have been made an overcomer and this satisfies my soul more than anything I could possibly own. Don't give up friend. The writer to the Hebrews calls us up with some powerful words of encouragement: "Don't throw away your confidence which has a great reward for you have need of endurance so that when you have done the will of God you may receive what was promised, for yet in a very little while he who is coming will come and will not delay, but my righteous one will live by faith and if he shrinks back my soul has no pleasure in him. But we are not of those who shrink back to destruction, but of those who have faith to the preserving of our souls." [Hebrews 10:35-39]

Stand up brother. With his hand of assurance on your shoulder re-enter the fight. God is a wise Commander-in-Chief and always knows when it's time for a little R& R. Trust his leadership and find your place in his ranks. A lot of people are counting on you. Stay far away from the swamp, choosing instead a lasting reward – it will come to you I promise.

AFTERWORD

Clearly, Jesus is the friend of sinners. He saw us when we were helpless and in bondage to sin, running in circles, without purpose, victims of the Evil One; we lived our lives in selfishness and unbelief until He intercepted us because of the great love with which He loved us. He called each of us by name and regenerated us by the power of the Holy Spirit. We are the recipients of free grace and eternally grateful for the blood He shed on our behalf. In closing this booklet I wish for each of us to *remember* how deeply Jesus loves sinners and no human soul is out of His reach. In support of this truth, we could perhaps consider any one of the many colorful characters presented to us in the Scriptures, men or women who were touched by Jesus and forever changed.

I've chosen to speak on behalf of Mary Magdalene because she, more than some of her male contemporaries, speaks on behalf of one like me – an orphan who was found and given residence with the King. Mary Magdalene demonstrates a devotion to Christ that is admirable beyond words. Real men treasure real women and I think you will be impressed with this woman's indomitable courage and her possession of faith.

We are first introduced to Mary Magdalene in Luke's Gospel Chapter 8. Let's begin here and then move around in the gospel narratives and beyond, seeking to understand the love Jesus lavished upon this woman as well as her response to God come to earth in the person of Jesus, an identity she discovered like many others who were eyewitnesses of His majesty.

You may already know there are many Marys mentioned in the Bible. It is thought that Mary Magdalene derives her name from Magdala which is small village that no longer exists. Archeological excavations reveal the village site was on the West side of the Sea of Galilee, and approximately 3 miles north of Tiberius. New Testament records reveal Jesus spent a great deal of time in this region, engaging people from all walks of life along the shores of the Sea of Galilee. "Jesus began going around from one city and village to another, proclaiming and preaching the kingdom of God. The twelve were with Him, and also some women who had been healed of evil spirits and sicknesses: Mary who was called Magdalene, from whom seven demons had gone out, and Joanna the wife of Chuza, Herod's steward, and Susanna, and many others who were contributing to their support out of their private means." [Luke 8:1-3]

Notice how the gospel writer introduces the men and women who shared regular fellowship with Jesus. Luke summarizes the twelve men with a single phrase and yet highlights each of the women by name: Mary Magdalene, Joanna and Susanna. We are told the specific manner in which they shared in Jesus' outreach to Israel, for they assisted the Lord in a very tangible way, contributing to the work from private means. In a time when women were seen as secondary citizens with no real voice in public matters, Jesus demonstrated a special interest and care for women[1].

I will offer you three things to consider – observations drawn from the life of Mary Magdalene. Let each of us hold tight to ourselves Mary's singular purpose for living. We might think of these as life applications. The first thing I notice is that Jesus became the center of this woman's world. As mentioned above, the bible tells us these women were healed of evil spirits and sicknesses. Following their encounter with Christ they could easily have thanked Jesus for His mercy and returned to life in their villages, but they were smitten with love for this man and could not imagine living for any other purpose than ensuring their Savior had ample resources to sustain Him and his disciples as they carried out the ministry of the Word – a ministry that was revolutionary, life-changing, soul-fulfilling and one for which there was no substitute.

You see, when a person is touched by Jesus, they become broken beyond repair in terms of ever fitting in again with the purposes of this world. The believer now has his or her sights set on heaven not on the things of this world. And, "They will mount up with wings like eagles,

---

1.   https://www.jesusfilm.org/blog/jesus-care-for-women/

they will run and not get tired, they will walk and not become weary." [Isaiah 40:31] These persons are strengthened because they have been given a new heart and never tire of involving themselves in God's Eternal Kingdom, which Jesus established when He arrived here, having been sent by His Father in heaven. When Mary Magdalene rose each day she didn't have to think through a long list of things to do. This woman had one purpose in life, following the love of her life, Jesus Christ. She rose, brushed her teeth, splashed some water in her face, and then grabbed a bagel, running straight away to join Jesus for a new day of adventure.

The second thing I notice is that Jesus became the center of her world. You read that correctly – second verse same as the first! There's a lot of speculation about Mary's background. Some scholars presume Mary Magdalene was the same Mary who wept at Jesus' feet as recorded in Luke Chapter seven, verses 36-50, where she is found drying His feet with her hair which would be a reasonable and heartfelt response to God for the mercy shown her. Moreover, many assume she was a prostitute or woman with a horrible reputation. But there really isn't any biblical basis for defining her specific sins; however, the New Testament does underscore her previous bondage, for the writer tells us Mary had seven demons cast out of her.

Whatever her background, we know she suffered at the hands of demons before meeting her Savior. But the bible doesn't define her according to who she was before meeting Jesus. All that matters is who she became after being found by Him. Jesus announced on one occasion, saying, "He who has been forgiven much loves much, but he who has been forgiven little loves little." [Luke 7:47] And isn't it true as we observe in life, "God has chosen the foolish things of the world to shame the wise, and God has chosen the weak things of the world to shame the things which are strong, and the base things of the world and the despised God has chosen, the things that are not, so that He may nullify the things that are, so that no man may boast before God." [1 Corinthians 1:27-29]

Mary is a supreme example of one who was likely despised by others prior to receiving Jesus' healing touch; I imagine she was likely lowly and weak, being in bondage to demons, suffering as a nobody amidst neighbors who could have nothing to do with someone so obviously cursed and abandoned by God. Mary became the object of God's mercy. Jesus saw this woman when everyone else was ignoring her. God sees you friend whether or not you're paying attention to Him. Jesus' stated mission according to Luke 19:10 reads, "For the Son of Man has come to seek and to save the lost." So, like Mary, we don't have to let our past dictate how we see ourselves. The apostle Paul explains it this way, "Therefore, if anyone is in Christ, they are a new creation, the old things are passed away behold all things are become new." [2 Corinthians 5:17]

Besides being healed by Jesus and following Him in ministry, John's Gospel tells us that she was one of the Marys present at the crucifixion. Near the cross of Jesus stood his mother, his mother's sister, Mary the wife of Clopas, and Mary Magdalene." [John 19:25]

I can't imagine the sadness that filled the hearts of these women as they stood a few meters from the cross on that first Good Friday. These women had been with Jesus, no less than the apostles of the Lord, serving Him and listening to Him for the better part of three years. What was going through Mary Magdalene's mind as she heard the hammers slamming nails into Jesus' palms and feet? What did she feel as she looked upon His frayed flesh, raw from the Roman style of scourging? The human heart is not designed to contain so much horror, sharing in Christ's apparent defeat.

A portion of my graduate studies included a three week study tour of the interior of Israel. One afternoon our class entered The Yad Vashem Holocaust Remembrance Center in Jerusalem where we observed six candles lit and many mirrors reflecting their light, representing the six million Jews killed during the holocaust. The portion of the building is nearly subterranean and feels like a morgue. During our visit to this Room of Remembrance we heard the names of men, women and children softly spoken via a hidden sound system, persons who suffered execution during a frightful time in human history when evil men of the Third Reich sought to annihilate an entire race of people – all the Jews living among them.

Yes, this is all horrifying to consider, but Mary Magdalene was contemplating something equally distressing, but far more profound: Jesus' mangled body was hanging suspended between heaven and hell; she beheld God's arms spread wide-open to an on-looking world, being held on the cross by thick steel spikes. We might imagine a single candle faintly glowing in Mary Magdalene's broken heart. Inside the morgue of her heart, she could only hear sadness and defeat as Roman soldiers went about their grisly work, crucifying three men on a dusty barren hill just outside Jerusalem.

Friends, there is a voice if we listen carefully in silence. Only one voice and only one Name is being considered here. Isaiah reports, "He was oppressed and He was afflicted, yet He did not open His mouth; like a lamb that is led to slaughter, and like a sheep that is silent before its shearers, so He did not open His mouth. By oppression and judgment He was taken away; and as for His generation, who considered that He was cut off out of the land of the living for the transgression of my people, to whom the stroke was due? His grave was assigned with wicked men, yet He was with a rich man in His death, because He had done no violence, nor was there any deceit in His mouth.But the Lord was pleased to crush Him, putting Him to grief; if He would render Himself as a guilt offering, He will see His offspring, He will prolong His days, and the good pleasure of the Lord will prosper in His hand.As a result of the anguish of His soul, He will see it and be satisfied; by His knowledge the Righteous One, My Servant, will justify the many, as He will bear their iniquities.Therefore, I will allot Him a portion with the great, and He will divide the booty with the strong; because He poured out Himself to death, and was numbered with the transgressors; yet He Himself bore the sin of many, and interceded for the transgressors."

[Isaiah 53] And as we know, Jesus didn't remain in the grave after He was executed. Because He is God, He rose from the grave on Easter morning victorious over Satan's realm, releasing all of us who call upon Him in truth.

The third thing I notice about Mary Magdalene is Jesus became the Center of Her World. Are you hearing an echo? And her devotion to Christ was rewarded by having been the first to witness our Savior alive from the grave. Mary was in fact the first evangelist of the resurrection, reporting to Peter and the others that Jesus was indeed alive, calling for them to meet Him in Galilee. Look at this extraordinary report from the Apostle John: "Now Mary stood outside the tomb crying. As she wept, she bent over to look into the tomb and saw two angels in white, seated where Jesus' body had been, one at the head and the other at the foot. They asked her, 'Woman, why are you crying?' 'They have taken my Lord away,' she said, 'and I don't know where they have put him.' At this, she turned around and saw Jesus standing there, but she did not realize that it was Jesus. He asked her, 'Woman, why are you crying? Who is it you are looking for?' Thinking he was the gardener, she said, 'Sir, if you have carried him away, tell me where you have put him, and I will get him.' Jesus said to her, 'Mary.' She turned toward him and cried out in Aramaic, 'Rabboni!'" [John 20:11-16]

I must draw your attention to a picture John offers us. Notice Mary observes two angels sitting in the tomb where Jesus' body had laid. One at the head and one at the feet. This is a living picture of the Mercy Seat that rests upon the Ark of the Covenant of God. As you might know there was ever only one place for atonement of the Nation's sins and that was at the Temple when the High Priest would enter the most Holy Place annually in order to sprinkle blood on the Mercy Seat on Yom Kippur – the Day of Atonement. The Mercy Seat features two mirror like angels with their wings extended covering the Ark of the Covenant. Here in the gospel of John, the author alludes to this sacred place by presenting us with a much holier site – the tomb of Christ – the place where Jesus' blood was spilled for the sins of the world. Two angels sent from God testify by their presence the solemn act of God for all ages – God did the unthinkable, and His satisfaction for sin has been met, bringing everlasting peace between Himself and men and women who have been redeemed by His amazing grace.

Recognize as well, Jesus' body is not found in the tomb. Mary fully expected to find Jesus' body laying on a stone bench inside. What an overwhelming experience for her to begin to absorb; *My Savior is gone and two men of an otherworldly nature are sitting here before me, pondering I assume, the great mercy of God for humankind.* The battle for our souls ended on Good Friday. Jesus rose from the grave for our justification, proving to all principalities and powers that He alone is God's Son – perfect in holiness and the only one qualified to make atonement for the sins of the world. Hallelujah, Christ is risen!

This is the most crucial event in history, and Jesus made a woman the first witness. He even sends her to tell the disciples what has occurred. [John 20:17] The irony is they don't believe Mary and the other women. Oh, the heart of this courageous woman, ignoring Roman soldiers and freshly spilled blood. Mary was too excited to worry over local law enforcement. As you can imagine, Mary must have been jumping up and down, turning summersaults, realizing the man she saw executed just a few short days ago was now standing before her calling her by name! If this were modern times and if Mary had driven to the tomb in her car she would likely have forgotten all about her car and run all the way home on foot before realizing she had abandoned her transportation back at the grave, so great was her joy!

Now, the last thing to notice is actually a personal question. Has Jesus become the center of my world? We talk a great deal about how important Jesus is, but where do I give Him room in my private world? When do I spend time with God when I'm not surrounded by other Christians? Have I taken time to stand before the cross at Calvary? Have I looked with dismay at Jesus' torn body, His nail pierced hands and feet. Have I ever felt the horror of Calvary and equally the horror of my sins for which He died? We must get beyond church talk about Jesus among friends. We must set aside time, indeed dedicate time, to speak to our own souls about the scandal of the cross. The scandal is this: I am a scandal. If newspapers printed and distributed the stories of my sins in all the awful details I would then know what it means to be a scandal in society. God became a scandal for me. Our holy God, Maker of heaven and earth took away my shame and clothed me with garments of righteousness because of His great love. The scandal of the cross also declares that every slap, thorn, nail and the lance by a spear into Jesus' side was required to cover my sins. I must realize that there is something profoundly wrong and out of tune in my heart, something only God could ever repair and this He did by sending Jesus the propitiation for my sins and yours, simultaneously regenerating those who put their faith in Him.

Mary Magdalene was very much in touch with these realities and made peace with God and *herself* through the cross of the Lord Jesus Christ. She brought the good news of Christ's resurrection to the Apostles, she brings you and me this good news today. How will we respond? This is a moment for each one of us to be still, turn our eyes to heaven and do business with God. Tell Him how you feel. John R. Stott is quoted as saying something to this effect: I myself could not believe in God apart from the Cross of Christ, for living in a world with so much suffering and pain; how could I believe in a God who was somehow immune to it? As you now know, God was anything but immune to the suffering of humankind.

Adam, the progenitor of the human race fell out of relationship with God because of his willful sin in the Garden of Eden. This is no fairy tale – far from it, for it is the grim story of evil's entrance to earth's stage and explains the lasting ramifications our parent's sin has had upon every person born into this world. Evil has disrupted our lives and relationships. I often hear the question asked, "If God is good, if God is real, if God is all powerful then why can't He be more preventative of evil? Why can't evil be contained?" These are legitimate questions that persons of every generation since Adam's expulsion from Eden have struggled to answer.

I'm reminded of God's conversation with Job, following his tortured experience at the hands of Satan. Job had questions and God responded by asking Job if he could explain a few realities from the *physical* side of the universe; Job was left tongue-tied. The upshot or conclusion of the matter is resolved near the end of the book of Job when we understand Job could not see and understand the *spiritual* side of the universe which was hidden from his eyes. God is not obligated to give us the full picture of His eternal purposes; however, we do see most clearly Jesus conquered evil, demonstrating His victory over death by rising from the grave. Mary understood the transaction: Jesus dying as a substitute for sinners. She understood the grave and demons and bondage and helplessness. Jesus heard her muffled heart cries; He confronted her enemies and took her from their cold clutches, delivering her from evil and making her one more of His own. God sees you. He understands you plight better than you do and He cares deeply about your welfare. We must come around and have a closer look at how God has dealt with evil, an evil that will one day be cast into the lake of fire. At that time we will not remember any part of our suffering here on earth, for we will have entered upon our eternal state, having received glorified bodies in which to dwell. In that day God promises to wipe away every tear from our eyes.

In closing I urge you the reader to dread the passing of Jesus. We do not know how often He might knock on the door of our heart. "So, working together with Him, we urge you (says the Apostle Paul), not to receive the grace of God in vain, for God says: At the acceptable time I listened to you, and on the day of salvation I helped you. Behold, now is 'the acceptable time,' behold, now is 'the day of salvation.'" [2 Corinthians 6:1,2]

"Scripture taken from the NEW AMERICAN STANDARD BIBLE, Copyright 1960, 1962, 1963, 1968, 1971, 1973, 1975, 1977, 1995 by the Lockman Foundation. Used by permission. www.Lockman.org[2]"

---

2.   http://www.Lockman.org

Conversations

<u>**Chapter 1, Introduction**</u>

A. Why do many men excel in their work, but often underperform relationally?

B. How does it feel to be "called up," by another man; resistance or excitement?

C. What is required to "call up" a person to his manhood?

D. Describe a man with meaningful relational involvement. How does he "show up?"

E. Do I feel any unique struggles, being a man, e.g. Memory Loss or Weightlessness?

F. How easily do we forget what is written?

G. What is it specifically that makes a man "weighty?" Not bricks in one's pockets.

<u>**Chapter 2, My Story**</u>

A. Can you describe your own story succinctly with a headline or two?

B. What course altering events marked your formative years?

C. Do you ever find yourself clinging to forms of shame that do not belong to you?

D. Respond to the apparent universal experience which states: life descends. Can this negative reality be met with positive energy or a redemptive response?

<u>**Chapter 3, A Road to Manhood Diagram**</u>

A. It has been said by persons of wonderful therapeutic experience, "Men who habitually get drunk don't do this to feel good, but rather to feel bad." Assuming this is true how do we explain this?

B. Only one Man has ever walked on water. How does this truth relate to the swamp?

C. What has been forgotten? Do you believe you are loved simply for who you are?

D. Does God offer men anything more alluring and soul satisfying than the swamp? Does He know our heart's desires? How does He offer to fulfill these?

Chapter 4, Where am I at Exactly?

A. Do you rely on any male models for direction who are of exceptional character?

B. Consider the question: How do others experience me?

C. Describe your process of integration as a human being.

D. Do you have a practice for daily recalibration of your internal compass?

Chapter 5, Travel Hazards

A. When's the last time you experienced a "road hazard?"

B. Jacob is described as a man who faced many "road hazards," yet he never failed to cling to God. How can we understand this man's faith to persevere?

C. How does shame affect a person's soul?

D. Do you know the difference between guilt and shame?

Chapter 6, Too Difficult

A. What does your graduation day look like? What will be required of you?

B. Why does the proverb tell us, "The eyes of a fool are on the ends of the earth?"

C. Does a stronghold with other men appeal to you as a sojourner in this world?

Chapter 7, Slippery Slope

A. Does "walking alone," afford us anything worthwhile?

B. Talk about assets and liabilities in terms of categorizing sacred treasure Vis a vis the purchase of cheap thrills that might actually cost a great deal of money. Name those that will appreciate over time and those that will lose value.

C. Why is it important to have a firm grip on who I perceive myself to be in relationship with others? Consider the power of fantasy, illusions of superiority and self-deception in your consideration of the slippery slope.

D. What's available to hold on to besides a brittle outcrop of a limb, protruding from the bank?

Chapter 8, The Swamp

A. How do men generally end up in the swamp? Do they walk directly to the marshland and dive in?

B. How does monotony contribute to swamp exploration?

C. What other lurid attractions might we find in the environs of the swamp?

D. Do you think it is possible to experience God in a way that makes the "pleasures" of swamp life utterly dull and uninteresting by comparison?

Chapter 9, Shattered but not Scattered

A. How does a man come to his senses when he has drifted so far astray?

B. Respond to the observation: Making friends with the imposter is the first step towards integration of body, mind, soul and spirit.

C. Is there more to consider when we suggest remembering *simply* brings the past into the present? Finish this thought however you choose: A man who fails to remember . . .

Chapter 10, Hey, I think I can

A. Explore the concept of intimacy between a man and a woman, seeing one another face to face. What does a woman desire from her man? Yes, to Provide, Pursue, Protect, but to be *Present* requires and inquisitive, daring heart!

B. How would you describe femininity in all its God-given glory?

C. Someone has said that a man and a woman's soul is the same shape as their sex organs. For example, men generally seek to penetrate their world, seeking to make a mark while women tend to console others, draw them in and arrange an environment for beauty and relationship. How can these divergent strengths praise one another?

<u>Chapter 11, Wow, Getting Traction</u>

A. Arriving home following an unauthorized absence. What are my expectations? How do you imagine the prodigal [described in chapter 15 of St. Luke's gospel], behaved after receiving complete reinstatement as a treasured son?

B. What is it in a man's chest that responds affirmatively to the question: Are you in danger of becoming a good man?

C. Faith, Hope and Love are unseen. How do we validate these virtues and make them manifest or real if you prefer?

<u>Chapter 12, Becoming a Man</u>

A. We've considered the consequences of leading a forgetful life. How can we train our minds as men to *Remember*? What practices are required?

B. Describe your present role as Prophet, Priest and King – your truth, intercession and rule.

C. In the movie: The Wizard of Oz, Dorothy awoke from a dream near the end of film and found herself back in Kansas surrounded by family and loved ones. What does this film's conclusion suggest to you?

POST SCRIPT

This book was conceived out of a personal ache in my heart, for young men I observe just getting started with responsibilities in life. I had no life map as a young person and few guides in terms of how to grow up as a man. There were a few choice men who reached out to me at various life stages, making a significant impact upon my overall trajectory. It's unlikely I would have ever written a booklet like this without their personal involvement and investment of time. My hope is many more mature men will step up to serve a sprouting generation, coming up behind us.

About the Author

Stan earned a B.A. in Biblical Studies at Trinity College and a Masters of Divinity at Trinity International University, both of which are located in Deerfield, Illinois. He completed a portion of his graduate studies on site in Israel. Stan has served as a pastor to single adults as well as an associate pastor in three different states over the span of more than ten years. He lives in Ohio with his wife, Theresa, with whom he has enjoyed 40 years of marriage. His previous publications include: News Among Jews in Chicago, Threading the Chicago Loop, Twelve Golden Monarchs and Loving Jennifer Tiles, each of which belong to his book series entitled: Water From a Rock.